Christ's Wounds
The Empty Tomb's Receipt

Poems of Suffering, Redemption, and Resurrection Hope

Drew Randolph

CROWN OF GLORY
Publishing

Published by Crown of Glory Publishing

Cover design: Drew Randolph
Interior design: Drew Randolph

Printed in the United States of America
First Edition

ISBNs
eBook – 979-8-9952091-0-2
Paperback – 979-8-9952091-1-9
Hardback – 979-8-9952091-2-6

Dedication

To all who carry suffering in their bones, who long for
relief, who search for hope when the night grows long.
To the hearts that ache for purpose and the souls
waiting to mend.
May these pages meet you where you are, and may their
words speak to you in love.
For in every valley, every question, every tear, we are met
by a Love far greater than we can comprehend…
a Love who steps into the fire with us, bears our sorrow,
and makes us whole again.

Death and the tomb are not the end but the room where resurrected new life begins.

— Romans 6:4, John 11:24-26, Luke 24:5-6

Table of Contents

Preface

Suffering is a language every human being learns, yet few of us ever feel fluent in it. We enter seasons we never asked for, carrying weights we never wanted, searching for meaning in the shadows. These poems were born in those shadows—in the places where questions rise faster than answers, where faith feels stretched thin, and where the heart aches for God to speak.

But suffering is never the end of the story.

Throughout Scripture, we encounter a God who steps into the fire with His people—the God who wrestles with Jacob, who walks with the three in the furnace, who weeps at Lazarus's tomb, who bears the cross none of us could carry. This book follows that same movement: from the ache of the human condition, through the breaking and the cry, into the turning where God draws near; and finally, toward the revelation of His glory.

Each section reflects a stage of the soul's journey:

- **The Human Condition** reveals our frailty and God's unchanging nature, as seen in poems like *Anchor in the Unchanging*.

- **The Descent** enters the rawness of suffering, where the heart bends, breaks, and begins to listen.

- **The Cry** captures the whispered prayers of the night—the surrender, the longing, the hope.

- **The Turning** unveils the God who steps into the fire with us, refining rather than destroying.

- **The Revelation** lifts our eyes to the glory that suffering cannot erase.

- **The Return** restores identity, wonder, and the truth of who we are in Christ.

- **The Call** invites us to live differently because of what the fire has formed.

- **The Benediction** leaves us with a hope that cannot be shaken.

These poems aren't meant to offer easy answers. They're meant to walk with you—to remind you that Christ is present in every valley, every question, every tear. As one poem declares, "Christ outweighs sorrow, bears our sin, His heavy mercy draws us in."

My prayer is that as you read, you will sense the nearness of the God who refines, restores, and redeems. May these words guide you toward the One who turns suffering into glory and ashes into beauty.

Sincerely—from the Latin sin-cera, meaning without wax, without pretense, not faking.

Sincerely,
Drew Randolph

The Human Condition— Where the Ache Begins

Anchor in the Unchanging

Time seems to slip faster as we age, reminding us how quickly strength fades. I hear it in the ticking of my mother's valve replacement and feel it in the daily rise and fall of diabetes, the energy crashes, and the exhaustion that comes without warning. Our bodies change, our days shift, and nothing we chase can outrun time. Yet these reminders turn our eyes to the One who does not change. God remains unshakeable and sure, the anchor who holds when everything else gives way, the constant who keeps us when time cannot.

Anchor in the Unchanging
We polish fading youth like silver losing shine,
Chasing dreams and cures and shadows, trying to outrun time.
The mirror turns storyteller, honest to the bone,
Etching lines like riverbeds where all our years have flown.

Knees creak like tired floorboards, breath thins like winter air,
Strength slips through trembling fingers, no matter how we care.
We taste the sting of changing days, feel memory's quiet drift,
Hear the ticking in our chest as every heartbeat shifts.
Seasons spin like turning wheels, relentless in their pace,
And we search for some illusion to hold still the human face.

But flesh is fragile pottery, cracking in the sun,
While You remain the mountain—unmoved, the only One.

Our words blow off like dandelions scattered in the breeze,
But Your Word stands eternal, untouched by time's decrees.
Treasures rust, empires crumble, even stars will dim and fall.
Yet You outlast the cosmos—the Maker of it all.

When storms of life grow violent and the world begins to shake,
When every earthly anchor snaps and every promise breaks,
Your faithfulness holds steady, a lighthouse in the roar,
A rock beneath the crashing waves, unmoved forevermore.

So, let the seasons change me, let time etch every line,
For I am held by One who does not age or bend or decline.
All things fade like breath on glass, all but One remain—
God, the everlasting constant, my anchor through the change.

And when the final season ends and time itself unwinds,
I'll rest in You unshaken—the One unchanged for all of time.

Numb Pain, Sin's Flame, and the Lord Beyond Pain

Suffering often drives us to anything that promises quick relief, and many of us learn to numb our pain rather than face it with God. We reach for distractions, habits, or comforts that quiet the ache for a moment but leave us emptier than before. The truth is that much of our hurt is shaped by our own choices, and we carry responsibility for the paths we take. Yet even in the pain we create, Christ waits beyond the numbness we chase. He is the only One who can meet us where the hurt begins and lead us to the healing we cannot find anywhere else.

Numb Pain, Sin's Flame, and the Lord Beyond Pain
Is pain a gift we're given to lift?
Where does a weary soul start to drift?
Purpose fades as sorrow sifts,
Life stands torn along the rift.
Chronic pain—numbness chased by a pill,
Lives slip away as hearts grow still.
Cost becomes the focus until
Death creeps close against the will.

Where can a soul find release from pain?
Sin leaves behind a dark, red stain.
Life is not loss but eternal gain—
Christ makes righteousness clear and plain.

When suffering rises, then wanes again,
A warning whispers: do not feed sin's flame.
Many blame God, yet truth remains—
Fault often bears our own name.

Life once dulled by pills and drugs,
A hallow ache no self can plug,
Christ's love endures, a truth that tugs—
A tender mercy that never shoves.
Christ calls us from self-made worth
To the promise of abundant birth.
The spotless Lamb paid a priceless cost—
A life restored, no longer lost.

The Consistency of Man, The Consistency of God

Life has a way of revealing how inconsistent we truly are. I see it in my own broken promises, in missed moments, in emotions that rise and fall without warning. I see it in friends who change, in children whose feelings shift by the hour, and in adults who are often no steadier than the youth they guide. Everywhere we turn, inconsistency marks our steps. When we fix our eyes on these shifting places, nothing in us can remain steady. Yet God stands unchanged. His constancy doesn't waver with our failures or our feelings. Only when we turn from the instability around us and fix our hope on the One who remains the same do we find the consistency our hearts long for.

The Inconsistency of Man, the Consistency of God
Oh, where does one start,
And where does one begin?
Where can we find a true, consistent friend
Amid the countless inconsistencies of men?

Inconsistency of man—how high they stand,
A rising tide across the shifting land.
Where to begin? The patterns only grow.
Inconsistencies surge with steady flow.
Teenage emotions rise, then fall again,
Changing so fast they puzzle full-grown men.
Joy blooms at dawn, then sorrow steals the day.
Yet sunrise brings new hope in gentle sway.

Hunger or pain—a baby cries in fear;
Inconsistencies mark their early years.
Tears stream like rivers down a tiny face,
Diapers changed at frantic, constant pace.

Children are told to try their best,
Yet countless distractions put them to the test.
Friends, toys, and sports that fade away;
They fall, they rise, never seeming to stay.

Desires of the heart shift like the tide,
Changing from youth until the day we die.
Waves crash and churn in ever-shifting play—
Inconsistencies mark our mortal way.

Sports show the same—missed calls and moments flawed;
Inconsistencies familiar to fans and squads.
It's the slip, the shock, the stumble in the fray,
That draws us to watch games each day,
For if perfection ruled each pass and play,
The thrill would fade, the wonder drained away.

Parents make vows to hold a steady plan,
Yet consistency slips from every hand.
Promises fade, and children feel betrayed;
Threats lose their weight when discipline decays.

Investments rise, investments fall in fear;
Some sell too soon, some hold and persevere.
Losses hit fiercely, like storms that rip the sails,
Chasing returns through storms and market gales.

Buildings reveal man's inconsistency too—
Each hammer strike, a little off, yet somehow new.
Paint strokes will vary, lumber swells with time;
Each cut tells stories in its shifting line.

Humanity's inconsistencies expand;
They follow man across the changing land.
No place he goes, no plan he dares to frame,
Escapes the faults that cling to Adam's name.
For man falls short in every plan he makes
And cannot match the strength God undertakes.

The weight of man's inconsistencies bows low
Before the God whose constancy won't slow.
Consistency anchored in one perfect plan —
Wrought by God's hand, not crafted here by man.
His sovereignty forever stands the same;
The Great I AM — unchanging is His name.
God's pursuit of us stays constant, firm, and sure,
While man's mind wanders, drawn to every lure.
Sin reveals the paths our hearts betray —
Man's inconsistency returns in full display.

We search for anchors strong enough to hold,
Pulling at threads of stories told of old.
But God's consistency will never bend;
Man's wavering ways in Him will find their end.

Perfect love shown in ways we can't explain —
On Calvary's cross, forgiveness still remains.

Holiness calls us from our broken mess;
God bids us walk in faithful steadfastness.
Man drifts through life on currents not his own,
But God stands firm — His strength and grace alone.

Seeded through generations long ago,
His promises continue still to grow.

The Trinity—unchanging, ever true;
Consistency in all He says and does and proves.

God's plan repairs the chasms deep and wide;
Scripture reveals the scarlet thread inside.
Letters in red shine mercy over dread—
Joy in His truth, not fear of what lies ahead.

Father, Son, and Spirit—Three in One;
Obedience called through Christ, the Holy Son,
Who came to rescue all, not just a few—
Consistent love made perfect, pure, and true.

Emotions rise and fall like shifting sand,
Yet God hates evil, loves with guiding hands.
Faith, hope, and love—His gifts that never sway;
Consistent blessings offered every day.

Miracles, wonders—His power revealed;
Prophets foretold, and Christ the promise sealed.
None of His words remain unmet or stayed;
Floodwaters rose, yet hope in Him remained.
The rainbow's brilliance, the promise God conveys,
His consistency through all our days.

Man's waywardness grows, his failures mound,
But God's firm constancy is always found.
His promises fulfilled, His grace made known—
Atonement through His Son forever shown.
Where man is frail and shifting as the sand,
God stands unchanging—holy, true, and grand.
Christ's constancy endures beyond all end;
He calls us into life with Him, our Friend.

The Mistaken Man and the Unmistakable God

We are far more mistaken than we care to admit. Our failures pile up faster than we can recount, yet most of us hide them, afraid to expose the cracks we carry. We cling to our mistakes in silence, holding the weight of them like baggage we never set down, and the despair only grows heavier. A. W. Tozer once wrote that only when he recognized his imperfections did he see his need for the One who is perfect. The same is true for us. Until we face our own flaws, we will never look for the God who has none. Christ meets us not in our polished moments but in the truth we finally confess; and in Him, we find the perfection our hearts have been searching for.

The Mistaken Man and the Unmistakable God

Man's mistakes are too many to recount,
A flood that rises past all measure or amount.
Each misstep carving stories of its own,
A path of thorns where sorrow's seeds are sown.

Shame, not glory, springs from every fall;
Man falters, stumbles—broken from the call.
Like refuse rising in a reeking mound,
Mountains of failures stretch beyond galaxies' bounds.
Most faults lie buried deep within the soul,
Locked in chambers where the heart grows cold.
The ground beneath begins to crack and break,
Under the crushing weight that every sin will make.

My imperfections cry out from within,
"Save me, Lord—I cannot conquer sin."
His shelves are lined with books that promise to renew.
Yet still his heart laments—no page can make him new
For self-help cannot heal the wounds no mortal hand can span;

Only Christ can touch the depth untouched by any man.

Where can he flee from faults that never cease their rise?
O wretched man, he groans within, as Paul once cried.
A contrite heart within him breaks, as David's psalm declares;
The Man of Sorrows bore the wounds his every sin prepared.
Worthy the Lamb, as heaven sings in Revelation's song —
The One who rights the wrongs that man has borne so long.

Mistakes become a weight he cannot bear,
Slowing his race, suffocating prayer.
Where can he flee from faults that never cease?
In himself he finds no refuge, no peace.

A Mount Everest of sin rises high,
A summit built beneath a fallen sky.
But if he knocks — if he will seek —
A door swings open, strong, yet meek,
And grace pours out, renewing the weak.

Only One walked earth without mistake;
Only One bore sin for mercy's sake.
Then the soul begins to rise and sing:
"Holy, Holy, Holy — worthy is our King."

Unmistakable truth resounds.
In God's living Word, hope is found.
Not empty speech nor hollow claim,
But living power in Jesus' name.

Christ came without blemish, without spot,
The Lamb fulfilling God's eternal plot.
He calls all men to seek His face —

To trade their ruin for His grace.

Christ — Kyrios, Messiah, Master, Lord —
By His blood, our peace restored.
The spotless Lamb, forever praised,
Unmistakable God in flesh displayed.

The veil was torn, the earth did quake,
Heaven rejoiced for redemption's sake.
The Spirit came to awaken man,
To bend the usurper to God's plan.

Now man, once fallen, kneels anew,
A supplicant made faithful, true.
From Genesis to Revelation shown,
God's flawless purpose stands alone.

Christ — Son of Man, the spotless Lamb revealed;
God's perfect plan fulfilled, no longer kept concealed.
Man's failures redeemed by the flawless One —
Our Savior, eternal reigning Son.

The mistaken man is made whole by the unmistakable God.

The Descent—When Suffering Breaks Us Open

Suffering's Seal Revealed

Suffering has marked my life in many ways. I was told I would never read well because of dyslexia. I endured physical abuse. I walked through retinal detachments and the sharp pain that comes with losing sight. I live daily with the ongoing challenges of diabetes and the exhaustion it brings. Most people will suffer in some way, whether through physical pain or the quiet weight of emotional wounds. Being alone doesn't shield anyone from suffering but often increases the load. Every parent knows the ache of hurting when their children hurt… a small reflection of how Christ comes alongside us and lifts us when we fall. Many feel suffering as a prison where hope seems locked away, and the questions of why me and why now echo without answer. Yet hope is found only where Christ spent His suffering. He meets us in the places we fear most and gives strength we cannot find on our own. In Him, the seal of suffering becomes the place where His mercy is revealed.

Suffering's Seal Revealed
Suffering—here we go again,
Pushed and shoved into a pit of pain.
No one escapes what suffering brings;

Where does sin cease to sting?

Suffering, the prison cell of the despondent,
Pain and hardship bending what once seemed constant.
Pain arrives—where does one lament?
Where the heart cries out and repents.
Hardness melts like dross when one relents;
Bitterness grows deeper when one resents.
Christ's love enters freely, heaven-sent;
Suffering's burden covered—love was spent.
Now we're called to walk the road Christ went.

Suffering draws us to a place destitute;
God strikes man's harp and softly tunes His flute.

Man seeks escape in self—oh, vain pursuit!
Christ, through death and atonement, plants love's root;

From buried seed, now breaking forth full-grown,
Grace lifts the soil where love is fully shown.
Suffering's cycle, a prison's rhyme,
Where many have pondered and wasted time.
Hearts imprisoned by invisible walls,
Fear of judgment, where every voice stalls.
Freedom breaks forth when testimony calls;
Only one Judge matters—eternal above all.

Affliction becomes a chance to draw near,
Pain falling like rain in sorrow's tears.
Our grief was borne by Christ through endless years;
One sorrow leads to worship through jeers.
Called before a cloud of witnesses and cheers,
Faith, hope, and love tested before strengthening peers.

Christ joins us in our trials; He knows the cost of our fall;
Where Christ broke into suffering for all,
Now we gain depth in sorrow's call.
Character forged, known to be love through all;
Christ broke down the barriers like Jericho's walls.
Praise God above for love that never ceases, never fails.

Christ looks upon us, cheering us on by His love;
God never drives His children with a push or shove.
The greatest gift poured out — far more than Noah's flood
Covered by Christ's love, by His — atoning sacrifice and blood.

Our suffering is like gold refined,
Stories carried forward, never left behind —
Proof of faith where love and hope unfold.
No one sells what love pours out; it shapes a life and forms
its mold.
Christ's love is the greatest story ever told,
Where suffering finds meaning in the Maker's love made bold.

The Purpose of Suffering

Most in Western culture believe pain should be avoided at all costs. Many worldviews teach that suffering is meaningless, an illusion to ignore, or a burden with no purpose. Christianity speaks with a different voice. Scripture tells us that Christ Himself suffered, and because He entered suffering, ours is never empty. No one escapes a life touched by pain, and character is often formed in the very places we would rather flee. When we look only at the hurt, despair grows, but when we look to Christ, hope rises in the midst of what wounds us. God shows us that suffering is not in vain.

His love sustains, shapes, and lifts us beyond the pit where
sorrow tries to keep us.

The Purpose of Suffering
Who can explain our suffering and pain?
Is sorrow brought only to shame?
Suffering—what is the cause of your claim,
A shadow returning again and again?

Suffering cracks the human heart,
No life escapes its painful start.
Some call pain experience, suffering choice,
Apathy rising to silence the voice.
If suffering is chosen, a burden we bear,
We search for a buffer, a breath from despair.

Can one live untouched by sorrow's name?
Isolation may shield, but life grows tame.
Alone, the ember cools to coal,
A fading fire within the soul.

Suffering humbles, brings us low,
A desperate cry for God to show
His presence near, His comfort true—
A holy friend who carries through.

Suffering—yet we are not alone,
Christ in His manhood fully shown.
Sin He bore for our soul's sake,
Unforsaken at the cross's wake.

Can love be known without the ache?
How shall a longing heart awake?
Where do we turn for suffering's worth?

Christ alone gives pain new birth.
His innocence pierced, His body torn,
Mocked, abandoned, crowned with scorn.

Apart from Christ, suffering stands bare —
No purpose, no meaning, no reason to share.
But in His wounds our hope is cast,
A love unbroken, unsurpassed.

Suffering has meaning in this life,
But glory ends all earthly strife.
No tear, no pain will still remain —
Christ heals our wounds and now sustains.

Paul learned joy through trials endured,
Perseverance grown, maturity secured.
Suffering now is not in vain,
Sin covered, life again reclaimed.
Love poured out, not weak or plain,
His life now flowing through our veins.

Where Sheep Fear, the Shepherd Draws Near

In Britain, shepherds guide their sheep through a plunge, a narrow trough of water that briefly submerges their heads to wash away parasites and disease. The sheep fear the moment they go under, yet the shepherd stays close and leads them through what they cannot face alone. When they rise from the water, the weight that once clung to them is gone. We are much the same. Pride, boasting, and the sins we carry cling to us like burdens we cannot shake, and we resist anything that humbles us. But where sheep fear, the Shepherd draws near. Christ guides His flock through what we dread, tending and mending us as He leads us toward freedom. In His care, fear loosens its grip, and we find rest in the One who calls us His own.

Where Sheep Fear, the Shepherd Draws Near
Sheep and herds at morning's begin,
Consecrated desire set apart from sin;
Parasites of suffering—no sheep's friend—
The sheep plunge deep so the plague may end.

Fear begins to rise ahead,
Where trembling sheep face pools with dread;
Yet suffering's purpose now comes through—
To cleanse from sin's old pest made true.
The Shepherd guides with staff and rod,
Reassuring faith on the path to God.

Suffering is where proud hearts stumble,
Where wavering souls may break and crumble;
Jacob strove with God through night's fierce press;
His voice still summons us to confess—
Truth we must not warp or suppress.

The sheep cry out in suffering's plea,
God calls His flock, "Return to Me."
The Shepherd, once hung on the tree,
Now by His Spirit lives in me.

Suffering marks the somber journey;
Judgment comes—who needs an attorney?
Christ, Physician and true Fisher of men,
Calls me His own, my eternal Friend—
The One who hears each whispered "Amen."

Head to the ground where we submit,
Crying, "Lord, hear the pleas we lament."
Christ's suffering stays forever relevant,
Faith, hope, and love His cornerstone cements.

The Shepherd tends His flock and mends,
Healing wounds, His mercy sends;
Guiding by His voice again,
The sheep walk on where grace attends.

Where do sheep grow strong the most?
Where suffering ends all earthly boast;
In Christ Jesus—never ghost—
Heaven rejoices with a celebratory toast.

The Cry—When We Reach for God in the Dark

Still, Lord, I Surrender

There are few pains like watching your child suffer. I remember the cries of my son begging not to face another needle, and the ache of knowing I had to allow what hurt him because it was for his good. Those moments stripped away every illusion of control. They brought me to the place where my own hopelessness had to rest in a hope outside myself. G. K. Chesterton wrote that hope in a hopeful state is mere flattery, but hope found in a hopeless state is the only hope of eternal worth. I learned that truth in the quiet desperation of a father's prayers. God was faithful and brought healing, yet the deeper lesson was surrender. Whether circumstances rise or fall, we are called to yield ourselves fully to the One who stands holy, glorious, and Lord of all.

Still, Lord, I Surrender
Why me? I asked in trembling despair,
Why now? My heart too burdened to bear.
"Take this cup," became my desperate cry,
But God said, "Lift it up—surrender to the Most High."

Still, Lord, I surrender all to Thee.

The weight felt far too heavy for my son to bear,
"Pour it on me, Lord—spare my heir."
But God replied, "This cup is his to carry through,
For in this trial, I will reveal My love to you."

Still, Lord, I surrender all to Thee.

"How, Lord, can this be?" I whispered in fear,
Yet still I prayed, "I surrender—I trust You are near."
This became my everlasting, soul-deep plea:
"Show Your will, O God—reveal Your hand to me."

Still, Lord, I surrender all to Thee.

And God, in mercy, chose to intervene,
A holy interruption by the Great I AM, unseen.
My son, a miracle—living, walking, standing tall,
A testimony that God still answers when we call.

Still, Lord, I surrender all to Thee.

His smile shines bright, a reminder each day
Of God's healing power and His sovereign way.
My righteous God, forever I worship Thee,
For who else offers love for all eternity?

Still, Lord, I surrender all to Thee.

The cup we bore has become the cup we share,
A witness of grace, of God's tender care.
His ways are not ours—thank God they stand alone,
For His strength moves where human strength is gone.

Still, Lord, I surrender all to Thee.

A touch of grace, a moment in His hour,
Natural met with supernatural power.
Only by God's nature and divine intention
Comes healing beyond human comprehension.

Still, Lord, I surrender all to Thee.

Glory to God on high —
All praises rising to His throne in the sky.
Turn our eyes to Him and gaze,
Bringing eternal glory, eternal praise.

Still, Lord, I surrender all to Thee.

Still, Your Light Leads Me On

Retinal detachment taught me how fragile sight truly is. When darkness closed in and vision slipped away, I realized how desperately I needed a light greater than my own eyes could give. Without light, we are all blind, no matter how strong our sight once was. In those moments of fear and uncertainty, Christ became the light that outshone my doubts. His presence rolled away the shadows that tried to settle over my heart and cast a renewing light that reached deeper than physical sight. His light does more than guide; it restores, it steadies, and it leads us back to Him again and again. Even when vision fades, His light remains sure, leading us on.

Still, Your Light Leads Me On
When sight grows dim, here we go again,
Losing vision, yet never losing a friend.

Still, I'm calling, following the light,
His lantern glowing in my longest night.

Still, Your light leads me on.

Bowing my head, not in fear or dread,
Walking in His light, His truth my daily bread.
Though eyes grow weak, I'm never alone,
Your steady glow has always shown.

Still, Your light leads me on.

The stone rolls away from my blinded eyes,
My spirit lifted, reaching toward the skies.
Like winter breaking into spring, I rise,
Cold once lay where warmth's love claims the prize.
Still, Your light leads me on.

O God, let a song rise up to You,
Lord, make our wandering hearts anew.
May the world behold how You came through,
No valley can keep us apart from You.

Still, Your light leads me on.

You cast off sin like east from west,
Removing the worst, restoring the blessed.
Oil overflows the font I am, without doubt—
Ensuring the fire will never burn out.

Still, Your light leads me on.

Face to the ground, humbled now,

At Christ's feet, alone I bow.

Still, Your light leads me on.

Author of Love Alone

Scripture tells us that we know love only because God first loved us (1 John 4:19). Christ showed us what true love looks like when He laid down His life, for there is no greater love than this (John 15:13). He came not to be served but to serve (Mark 10:45), calling us friends and drawing near with a love that doesn't falter (John 15:15). His resurrection reminds us that His love is not bound by death or time (Matthew 28:6), and His friendship doesn't end at the grave. Every act of Christ reveals that He is the Author of love alone, the One who defines love, gives love, and sustains love. In Him, we learn what love truly is and who we are called to become (Romans 5:8).

Author of Love Alone
Before the dawn of dust and breath,
You knew our lives, planned to conquer death.
We ask in wonder how we came—
Formed by Your love, called by Your name.

This tongue of mine, both praise and flame,
Speaks blessing, then betrays Your name.
A restless fire, a caged desire,
Yet love can quench what once burned fire.
Then lips redeemed will rise and sing
Of glory bright in You, our King.
You teach: our war is not with flesh
But sin within that fights afresh.

A battle deep no eye can see—
A wounded heart that longs to flee.
So, Spirit, come and dwell in me;
Break chains that bind, set captives free.

From Eden's grief, when shame first fell,
You clothed the pair who knew it well.
The first spilled blood, a covering made—
A shadow cast, a promise laid.
A sacrifice to hide their sin,
A whisper of the Lamb to win.

O wretched self that strives within,
Still wrestling with the weight of sin—
Cast off the flesh, let Spirit reign,
For Paul declared we die again.
Each day we lay our lives before
The One who opened heaven's door.

You gave the offering first, O Lamb,
A sacrifice for every man.
The cross—Your love in crimson poured,
The final covering now secured.
What Eden hinted, You fulfilled;
The spotless blood, the Father's will.
Now You, O Christ, are all our worth,
The treasure heaven sent to earth.

You melt my heart, You draw me in;
Your Spirit dwells where death had been.
I dare not cast aside the gift
You bought with blood to heal and lift.
So, make my heart to You inclined—

Soft, surrendered, wholly Thine.

This will remain my constant plea:
To love the One who first loved me.
My life, my breath, my hope, my own —
To You, Author of Love Alone.

Never Forgotten

Who can comprehend the mind of God or the depth of His memory? We forget names, moments, promises, and even the people we love, but God forgets nothing that He has set His love upon. One of the greatest fears of the human heart is to be overlooked or forgotten, yet our greatest need is to know that God remembers us. Scripture tells us that He has engraved us on the palms of His hands and that not even a sparrow falls without His notice. In a world where memories fade and people drift, God's remembrance is steady and sure. To be held in His mind is to be held in His mercy, and to be remembered by Him is to never be lost.

Never Forgotten
To whom do we pray, whom we dare not forget?
In whom do we hope, whose promise is set?
Called by the Father, Christ entered our night —
Oh, how we reach for His garment of light,
Never forgetting the cost Christ's blood made right.

Man longs to be lifted from ruin and shame,
From depths where he cries out to God in his pain.
Satan cannot move God from His rightful throne,
Nor steal the dominion that man once owned.
So, God came as man, His mercy made known —

Living water poured out, Holy grace sown.

How can we be cared for, remembered, restored?
Only through Christ, in a life fully poured.
Our memories falter, our thoughts drift away;
Hours and minutes fade through the course of a day.
Yet Christ brings hope to the hearts led astray.

How much can one mortal mind truly keep?
How many truths can be buried so deep?
Our thoughts are fragile, limited, small,
Yet God shaped each mind with brilliance for His call.
His wisdom stands firm where our memories fall.

Where does the vessel of memory end?
Man's reaches its limit, unable to extend.
But God's endless knowledge forever ascends —
We lean on His Spirit, our Helper and Friend,
Whose guidance sustains us from start to the end.

So what should the longing of mankind be?
Never forget what Christ did on that tree.
Let sovereign love shape the heart and the mind,
Glory assured for the chosen, refined,
Held in remembrance by God ever kind.

Lord, we bow humbly before Your great seat;
Your memory vast, You remember Your sheep.
Christ intercedes, His remembrance our plea —
Grace and mercy flow, preserving the weak,
Love crying out for the souls He will keep.

God's memory holds every moment and day;

He numbers our steps and guides all our ways.
His promises stand, His covenants stay —
Christ came proclaiming God's power displayed,
In Him we are kept, not lost or afraid.

God's memory — eternal, faithful, and kind —
The deepest desire of all humankind.
How can mere mortals this mystery find?
Never forsaken, in Christ we're aligned,
Held in His heart and eternally signed.

Praise to the Savior who sought and who found,
Breaking the chains where our sins were once bound,
Beyond the pounding weight of sin and shame,
Grace and mercy cover all in His name;
Kneeling in awe, my heart resounds —
Glory to God, whose memory abounds.

The Turning—God Steps into the Fire within Us

Refined in Suffering

There are moments when suffering presses in from every side and the fire feels too hot to endure. I remember facing a neuroanatomy final with less than a day to prepare, all while knowing retinal detachment surgery was waiting for me on the other side of the exam. Fear, exhaustion, and uncertainty closed in like flames, and I had nothing left to stand on but a cry for help. Yet it was there, in the heat of that moment, that Christ walked with me. Scripture shows that God doesn't keep His people from the fire; He steps into it with them. The same Christ who stood with the three in Babylon's furnace stood with me in my own. Suffering becomes the place where God invites us to call out to Him, where our strength ends and His begins. In the fire, we are not abandoned. We are refined, upheld, and made new by the One who never leaves us in the flames alone.

Refined in Suffering
What is our suffering in this time?
A whisper of Solomon's fleeting rhyme.
A humble call, a cry to God,
Whose glory shines where saints have trod.

Suffering—the refiner's fire of joy,
Shaping, molding, not meant to destroy.
Burning away the dross within,
Revealing Christ where we begin.

Not fully known without the flame,
Yet God walks with us, calls our name.
His Word breathes life, His truth inspires,
His holy presence in the fires.
What flame can claim what He redeems?
What death can shame His risen beams?
Suffering reveals His glory bright,
A binding love, eternal light.

Grief and sorrow are not ours alone—
Christ, who suffered most, now reigns above.
The greatest gift of suffering still is love,
He fills our sails with hope from heaven's throne,
Our trials make His character known,
Draping our suffering in His mercy shown.

So, if suffering calls, may I still run,
Endure the race until it's done.
Paul shows the strength that faith can face,
A steady stride toward heaven's embrace—
Christ interceding in my place,
His grace sustaining every pace,
Until I meet Him in His radiant grace.

The pendulum swings with questions deep,
Why must we suffer? Why must we weep?
Christ outweighs sorrow, bears our sin,
His heavy mercy draws us in.

He calls the widow, the orphaned child,
The lost, the lonely, the reconciled.

Through every trial, every pain,
God's glory still eternally reigns.
A light in darkness always shone,
His presence near in valleys known.
Where pride must fall, our hearts grow meek,
His mercy meets the worn and weak,
And suffering bows where Christ we seek.

Christ came as bridegroom, love made whole,
Never leaving the suffering soul.
The curtain torn, eternal bloom,
First fruits rising from the tomb.

Suffering tells redemption's story—
The cross, the grave, His risen glory.
Scripture filled with human cries,
Yet Christ, the Son of Man, will rise.
Injustice groans, but joy will stand—
Every knee bows at His command.

Why do we suffer? Christ makes it clear:
Our pain brings God's eternal purpose near.
Refined in suffering, shaped by His design—
We rise in love as God refines His own.

Holy, Holy, Holy—glory to God alone, divine.
Glory is Yours; all crowns are rightly thine.

Light That Breaks Our Tomb

RC Sproul once spoke of how we stumble through life by the flicker of a candle, seeing only shadows and outlines, never the full truth. C. S. Lewis used the same image, reminding us that we grope through the rooms of our lives with dim light, until the curtains are thrown open and daylight floods in. That moment of sudden brightness is what the resurrection brings. We are called to realize that a new dawn has broken upon us, that hope has risen with Christ, and that the light of His life has shattered the darkness of death. I once feared what lay ahead, but the light Christ brought into my soul rolled away that fear. His resurrection is not only true in history; it's true in me. The light that breaks our tomb is the light that leads us home. How wonderful it is to have found You, Christ (John 1: 5, Romans 6:4, Ephesians 5:14).

Light That Breaks Our Tomb

In darkness we wander, repeating our fall,
Lost deep in the shadows, stuck fast in a stall;
Yet Christ in His mercy, the sinless, the true,
Breaks into our night with a radiance new.

We stumble by candle, its flicker so slight,
But heaven bursts open with unborrowed light;
The curtain is parted, the Holy made near,
And songs fill the chamber where once dwelt our fear.

O marvelous brightness that sweeps through the room,
It scatters the shadows and silences gloom.
Our cup, once in darkness, now brims with His grace,
His love overflowing in every place.

Creation awakens with colors He cast,

Each beam of His glory redeems what was past.
The heavens reflect Him, the earth joins the cry,
And praise rises upward like incense on high.

Though trials may linger and storms may arise,
His light is our banner, our strength, and our prize;
No darkness can hold us, no shadow consume—
For Christ walks before us, the Lord of the tomb.

So, shine in my spirit, O Light from above;
Restore what was broken and fill me with love.
From cave into sunrise, my soul You renew—
By Your risen splendor, I see all things true.

His Wounds, the Tomb's Receipt

Few moments in Scripture carry the weight of Thomas placing his hand into the wounded side of the risen Christ. Jesus stands before him, scars still visible, and Thomas can only cry out, "My Lord and my God" (John 20:28). That confession is not a simple statement. It is the breaking open of a soul that suddenly sees the truth. It is the moment when doubt collapses under the weight of glory. Christ didn't hide His wounds from Thomas. He invited him to touch them, to feel the proof of a love that suffered, bled, and rose again (John 20:27).

It is the same for us. The deepest transformations in our lives often come when Christ touches us with His scars. His wounds speak a truth our hearts cannot deny. They proclaim who He is, Lord and God, and who we become when we believe. His scars aren't symbols of defeat but the very marks of victory. They are the receipt of the empty tomb, the evidence that the debt of sin has been paid in full. Scripture declares that Christ canceled the record of debt that stood against us, nailing it to the cross (Colossians 2:14). Nothing can be added to His work and nothing can be taken away. The sacrifice is complete. The tomb is empty. The payment is finished.

When we echo Thomas's words, we join the greatest proclamation a human being can make. We declare that Jesus Christ is Lord, that His suffering wasn't wasted, and that His resurrection is the glory that now defines our lives. His wounds shine with the light of redemption, and His risen life calls us to worship, to trust, and to stand in awe. In His scars, we see the truth of our salvation and the glory of the One who paid our debt completely.

His Wounds, the Tomb's Receipt
Trials rise in countless shapes and sizes,
Like storm-tossed ships that tilt as one capsizes.
We sway, we strain, yet still the truth is clear:
What can be learned when heavy trials draw near?

We cannot choose each path our feet must tread,
But we choose every word and step instead.
The road before us isn't always ours to choose,
And plans built on our strength are ones we often lose.
Comfort, though sweet, can make the spirit weak,
But trials refine the strength of those who seek.
For God begins His work in fire and test,
And those who walk the trial find deeper rest.

We're told to glory in our suffering's weight,
For perseverance grows through every ache.
Endurance shapes the heart where faith is found,

And Christlike character resounds and abounds.

A living hope is His alone to give,
A love that died and rose so we might live.
We seek our Lord—our Shepherd, Savior, Light—
Who dwells with us and holds us through the night.

The spotless Lamb, who bore God's perfect plan,
Entered our ruin, standing in the place of man.
His wounds are the empty tomb's receipt—
Proof that the debt is paid, the work complete.
A steadfast hope not built on works we've done,
For Christ accomplished what we could not become.

He paid the price—He holds the tomb's receipt;
Through Him, our ransom stands forever sealed and complete.
Purchased by grace, we fall before His face,
Upheld by mercy, wrapped in love's embrace.

God's steadfast mercy pours from heaven above,
A gift of unending, faithful, firm in love.
In Christ, we stand as heirs, redeemed and friends—
A love unbroken, a life that never ends.

So, what do we lack? In Him, nothing at all.
Count every trial joy, for Christ has called.
By mercy's strength we rise; in Him we stand,
For Christ upholds our steps with sovereign hand.
What do we learn when storms stretch mile by mile?
To walk the way of Christ—beneath His never-ending smile.

Scripture References: Romans 5; James 1; 1 Peter 1; Isaiah 53:5

The Revelation—Glory in the Midst of the Fire

Glorious Weight Shown

The story of God's glory stretches across Scripture in a movement both ancient and new. In the Old Testament, the word for glory is *kavod*, a word that means weight, heaviness, and substance. It speaks of the sheer gravity of God's presence, the God whose nearness caused mountains to tremble and whose voice shook the wilderness. His glory was a weight no human could bear apart from His mercy.

In the New Testament, the word shifts to *doxa*, a word that carries the sense of radiance, splendor, and beauty revealed. What was once known as weight becomes known as wonder. The glory that once rested like a cloud on the tabernacle now shines in the face of Jesus Christ. He carries the fullness of God's *kavod* in the splendor of His character, His compassion, His obedience, and His sacrifice. The weight of God's glory becomes visible in the life of the Son, and the splendor of God's glory becomes undeniable in His resurrection.

Christ doesn't merely reflect God's glory; he embodies it. He bears the weight of divine holiness and reveals the beauty of divine love. In Him, the heaviness of God's presence and the radiance of God's splendor meet. The cross shows the weight of glory carried for us, and the empty tomb shows the splendor of glory revealed to us. Through Christ, we behold the fullness of God's glory, both weighty and wonderful, both humbling and exalting. In Him, the glory of God is not distant but displayed, not hidden but shown, not feared but adored.

Glorious Weight Shown
Weight of Glory—ancient Kavod,
Heaviness where heaven showed.
Man can't lift nor struggle through—
Who can measure the weight of You?
For You disclose what's ever true,
The God who breaks and builds anew.

No scale comes close to estimate,
No mind can grasp such holy weight.
The glory man cannot unveil,
Yet, still, Your patience will prevail.

Where does weight begin to matter?
Where sin lies heavy on the platter.
A life that trembles in the balance,
God's weight outshines all human talents.
Man's weight swells as sins grow greater;
God's weight of glory makes scales shatter.
Who can stand alone, unshaken?
His glory mends what man forsaken.
Only Christ's shoulders bore the weight,
A burden no man's strength could take.

Weight of God's glory—timeless, old,
Splendor prophets long foretold.
Then came doxa, brightest splendor,
Calling forth our full surrender.

Christ—pure character unrolled,
Judgment just, yet grace untold.

Where does weight meet holy splendor?
Where Christ invites our full surrender.
Eternal glory now awaits,
Shown to us true, not to forsake;
Christ calls, speaking truth to take.
Praise Christ the Light for mercy's sake,
He bore the burden, paid the price;
His blood alone the sacrifice.
No work of man could e'er suffice;
Praising God's only begotten choice,
Through Him we hear the Mediator's voice.

What then will your heart choose?
Man's own weight is sure to lose.
Pride bows low beneath sin's bruise;
Christ calls—His love the fuse
No weary soul can long refuse.

Three in One—no glory undone,
The weight of heaven in the Son.
Christ's eternal love, the radiant One—
Trinity reigning, victory won.

Vision in His Rising Light

During retinal detachment repair, I spent long hours lying prone, face down and still. The world narrowed to silence and waiting, and in that stillness, I discovered a different kind of sight. When everything else was stripped away, the quiet voice of God became clearer than ever before. Physical vision was uncertain, but His spiritual light remained steady. His light doesn't dim with fear or circumstance. It rises over every shadow and reveals His presence in ways we often miss when life moves too quickly. In the quiet, I learned that His light is the truest vision of all, a light that remains bright regardless of what the day may yield.

Vision in His Rising Light
I lay prone through long-healing days,
Softly singing Amazing Grace.
Retina mending, sight incomplete —
The cost still blurred, yet His touch is sweet;
He guides my steps, He steadies my feet[1].

Three days of wonder, three of rest,
Christ lifting sorrow from my chest.
Though weakness made me lay down my might,
His mercy raised me in His light[2],
A quiet strength through every night.

Passover's Lamb, the Holy One[3],
Walked toward the cross, God's willing Son.
Riding in low on humble frame[4],
The crowd cried out to curse His name,
Yet still He bore our guilt and shame[5].

Pontius asked what wrong He'd done —

But innocence was true; He was the One
Anointed pure, without a stain[6],
Who carried every human pain,
So none would wander lost again[7].

At dawn He rose, the grave undone[8],
A brighter hope than morning sun.
The stone rolled back, death lost its claim[9],
And every heart that calls His name[10]
Finds resurrection in His flame.

Now, as my sight returns in part,
A deeper vision fills my heart.
The Holy Spirit brings great light[11],
Reveals the Lord in holy might,
And grants the soul its truest sight[12].

He shapes the view within my soul,
Corrects the lens, restores the whole.
Not just the eyes that face the day,
But inner sight along His way[13] —
A clearer path, a brighter ray.

Ever welcoming, soft and bright,
He draws me toward His endless light[14].
Though eyes are blurred, my spirit sees
The risen Christ who whispers peace[15]
And calls my vision into ease.

Yet greater still the sight to come —
When earthly shadows all grow numb.
For God Himself will fill my view[16],
A glory vast, a brilliance true,

The final focus breaking through.

The Spirit leads in steady ray[17],
Preparing me for heaven's day.
Where faith dissolves in perfect light[18],
And God on high is my delight —
The everlasting, fullest sight.

Footnotes (Scripture References)
1. Psalm 37:23
2. 2 Corinthians 12:9
3. John 1:29
4. Zechariah 9:9
5. Isaiah 53:5
6. Hebrews 4:15
7. Luke 19:10
8. Matthew 28:6
9. 1 Corinthians 15:55
10. Romans 10:13
11. John 16:13
12. Ephesians 1:18
13. Psalm 119:105
14. Revelation 21:23
15. John 20:19
16. Revelation 22:4
17. Romans 8:14
18. 1 Corinthians 13:12

The Return—Identity Recovered Through the Fire

Man's Wander, Returned to Wonder

From the moment Adam stepped outside the garden, humanity began to wander. His drift wasn't only a movement of feet but a movement of the heart. Adam was created to wonder at God, to live in awe of the One who formed him, yet he turned his attention to creation instead of the Creator. What began in him continues in us. We ponder the world, analyze its beauty, and chase its mysteries, yet we often forget to lift our eyes to the God whose breath brought it all into being.

We were made to wonder, not wander. When wonder fades, the heart grows weary. When awe is lost, the soul begins to drift. But God meets our weariness with a love that is tender and calls us back to Himself. He invites us to return to wonder, to recover the holy amazement that awakens worship and restores our vision. True wonder doesn't end in creation; it leads us to Christ. In Him, the Creator steps into creation, and the One we were made to behold becomes the One who calls us home. When wonder returns, so does worship, and every wandering heart finds rest in the God who alone is worthy of awe. All who see Him can only say amen.

Man's Wander, Returned to Wonder

God called our hearts to holy wonder,
Yet Adam chose instead to wander;
He stepped away to think and ponder,
And left the garden's peace asunder.

Mankind grew lost in what it cost,
Through storms of heart, we're tossed;
In every ache, in every loss,
We feel the line our footsteps crossed.

The mind now turns like gears that rust,
Wandering paths that fade to dust;
Yet in our awe, in God we trust—
For wonder calls us back from dust.

From wandering far, we're called to return,
To ask what truth our hearts must learn;
His Spirit flames so none are burned,
A holy fire for which we yearn.

The Spirit descends like a gentle dove,
Heaven's gift from realms above;
Christ—whom angels sing of—
Meets our wonder with His love.

For God does not wonder what He'll do,
No guessing, doubting, thinking through;
The Trinity stands—three, not two—
Perfect knowing, perfect view.

So, man returns again to ponder,
Finding grace wrapped in holy splendor;

Where weary hearts in awe surrender,
And love meets wonder, soft and tender.

The Call—
Life After the Fire

Final Call

As Jesus hung on the cross, a dying man beside Him offered a final plea. He had nothing to bring and no time left to change his life, yet Christ received him even in the midst of His own suffering. While bearing the weight of the world's sin, Jesus still turned toward a sinner's cry and answered with mercy. His promise, "Today, you will be with Me," shows that it is never too late to turn to Him. Christ meets us not after the pain has passed but right in the heart of it, joining us in our suffering just as He did that day. The thief's surrender reveals a truth that stands for every generation: His final call is offered to us all, and every honest cry is met with the fullness of His grace.

Final Call

Where does one face the final call?
On a cross raised high where shadows fall.
Each breath a climb, each rise a crawl—
Yet Christ remembers, Lord of all.

Never too late in life's short span
To lay down flesh, forsake its plan.
Call Jesus Lord, trust God's command—

Love proved in nails through Savior's hands.

God on the cross
Draws near the lost:
Widow and orphan, feeling tossed.
Christ paid the price our sin had cost.

He met the weak, the cast aside:
Moses drifting with the tide,
Abraham waiting, faith his guide,
Job refusing friends who lied,
Jacob lifted, justified,
Noah building though denied,
Daniel faithful though defied,
Three in the furnace — God beside.

The cross bore witness as He died;
One name alone we testify.
The empty tomb now stands to verify
The Holy One who sanctifies.

God whispers close in moments grim;
Pain sharpens how we hear from Him.
Our trembling hearts grow still and dim —
Eternal life flows out from Him.

Christ whispers soft as He draws near,
Mercy tender, eyes sincere.
He calls us home beyond the years —
Adoption sealed as heaven cheers.
On cross or bed, you still may find
Sin's grip like chains around the mind.
Surrender all, leave death behind;

Call Christ your Lord—true rest you'll find.

Conviction lights the brand-new start;
No more the weight of sin's old cart.
Receive the Savior in your heart;
His Spirit grows in every part.

So, the question still remains:
Will you call on Christ's holy name?
Life transformed—never again the same;
The Spirit ignites the soul with flame.
New birth, new life—Christ stakes His claim.

Where Suffering Finds Its Home

We all know the truth Scripture declares—that if we say we have no sin, we deceive ourselves. Our lives bear the marks of wandering hearts and weary souls, and in that weariness we long for someone who will not leave us. Job felt the same ache. His friends couldn't save him, and he cried out for a mediator, someone who could stand between God and man. We share that same need. We cannot rescue ourselves, and no human companion can carry the weight of our suffering. Yet God has given us a home in Christ Jesus, the true Mediator and faithful Friend. He calls us brothers and sisters, and He welcomes us with a love that doesn't end. In Him, our suffering finds its place, and our longing finds its rest.

Where Suffering Finds Its Home
Humbly brought low once again,
Desperate pleas cry out for a friend.
Prison of darkness where all have sinned—
Do not leave me in the abyss without end.

One laments with downtrodden cries,
Too young, too wounded, too many lies.
Who breaks sin's grip and gently pries?
Humanity without hope surely dies,
Never to look upon Holy eyes.

Suffering in shadows with no light to see;
Life must be found outside of me.
Suffering alone—how deep the ache can be.

Where can a soul find a path to be free?
Only one place: the incarnate on a tree,
Calling humanity, "Come unto Me."

Suffering has purpose, not terror or fear;
Sin's subtle evil draws ever near.
Satan whispers his lies and sneers,
But Love pierces like a sharpened spear—
Proof of the sacrifice calling us dear.
Many behold as hearts are changed here;
Praise God for love beyond mortal years.

His abundant love, perisseuō, overflows;
Innocent suffering fully shows.
Where holiness burns and mercy glows,
Understanding fails, yet compassion grows.

Our scars of suffering are not borne alone;
"My Lord, my God," cried Thomas with a groan.
He gives us cause to praise Heaven's throne—
Suffering ends where Heaven is home.

Triumphant Victory and Consecration to Christ Our King

We are called to lift our voices in psalms of praise and give glory to Christ our King for all He has done, all He is doing, and all He will bring to completion. His promises stretch from yesterday into today and flow into eternity, each one secured by His triumph. Our joy is found in Him alone, for nothing apart from God's own throne can satisfy the longing of the human heart. In worship, we consecrate ourselves to the King who reigns in victory; and in praise, we join the everlasting song that rises to the Lamb who is worthy forever.

Triumphant Victory and Consecration to Christ Our King

Sing, O soul, the Savior's name,
Lift His glory, spread His fame.
From the cross, His mercy flows,
Life eternal Christ bestows.

Mountains bow, the stars proclaim,
Heaven echoes Jesus' reign;
Love unmeasured, vast and free,
Binding hearts eternally.

Take my life, O Lord divine,
Every breath shall now be Thine.
Hands and heart to Thee I raise,
Consecrated in Thy praise.

Death defeated, grave undone,
Victory shines through God's own Son;
Crown Him now, the risen King,
Joy forever let us sing.

The Benediction—Hope That Cannot Be Shaken

The Anchor in a World that Shifts

The world never stops shifting. It moves from one fad to another, from one opinion to the next, always changing and never settled. Minds drift, foundations crumble, and nothing holds steady for long. No anchor the world could create can keep a soul from drifting. We remain restless until we fasten ourselves to what doesn't change. While everything around us rises and falls, Christ remains the same. Jesus is Lord, Creator, and the sure foundation beneath every trembling heart. In a world that cannot hold its shape, He alone is the anchor that holds fast.

The Anchor in a World That Shifts

Waves keep tossing me to and fro,
And still I wonder which way to go.
Blown like chaff in a restless wind,
Searching the world for a faithful friend.

Choosing dinner becomes a quest—
Tacos? Burgers? I second-guess.
Every choice becomes a fight;
I drift again before first bite.

Too many brands on every stand,
Too many apps to overplan.
Should I work out, nap, or scroll?
My mind's a hamster on a roll.

We switch our hobbies every week,
Buy gadgets "new," then lose the streak.
We change our houses, change our hair,
Change our shoes, because we can't compare.

We chase upgrades we'll never keep,
Promises big but shallow and cheap.
Life becomes a frantic spin —
Anchored in nothing but passing whims.

But when the noise grows loud and wild,
And my thoughts run off like a scattered child,
A still small voice breaks through the storm —
A love unchanging, steady, warm.

The One whose constancy is a gift,
The Anchor firm when storm winds shift.
The Rock of Ages — sure, secure —
The Cornerstone, our Anchor evermore.

He calms the winds that shake my soul,
He draws me near and makes me whole.
Though all the world may fade or bend,
His steadfast love will never end.

And though my thoughts may drift and roam,
In Him, my restless heart finds home.
No tide can pull, no storm can sever —

The God who holds me holds forever.

When all around me shakes like sand,
His Word remains, His promises stand.
My hope is fixed, my fears undone—
Anchored in the Unchanging One.
Held fast within His grace above,
Rooted deep in redeeming love.
The shifting world may rise and fall—
But Christ the Lord is Lord of all.

Eternal Tomorrow

This poem is dedicated to Penny McHenry, a beloved woman who walked through the valley of cancer with grace and quiet strength. Even as her body weakened, her faith remained steady, and her light continued to shine in the growing community of believers who loved her. I wrote this poem after my retinal repair, carrying my own questions and pain, yet thinking of the hope she held so firmly. Penny's life reflected a radiance that touched everyone around her, a light that didn't fade even as her earthly tomorrow drew near its end. Her eternal tomorrow in Christ was already secure, and her legacy remains, because she went home to the One who is the source of every shining life.

Eternal Tomorrow
In Your ever-present story,
He reigns in eternal glory.
Through trials that cloud the day,
His light will never fade away.

Do not despair in your present sadness,

For Christ will bring eternal gladness.
Though shadows linger, hope will rise—
A promise shining through the skies.

We do not dwell on our present sorrow
But give Him praise for tomorrow—
A bright future, where tears shall cease,
In Christ, eternal joy and peace.

For in His resurrection power,
New life blooms like the morning flower.
The grave defeated, death undone,
Our hope secured in God's own Son.

Dedicated to Penny McHenry,
a woman who continues to live on in paradise.

Scripture Reference Index

New Testament

Matthew
– *Christ's call to surrender—Still, Lord, I Surrender*

Luke
– *"Why do you seek the living among the dead?" (Luke 24:5–6)—Epigraph*

– *Christ's nearness in fear—Still, Your Light Leads Me On*

John
– *"I am the resurrection and the life" (John 11:25–26)—Epigraph*

– *The Good Shepherd (John 10)—Where Sheep Fear, the Shepherd Draws Near*

– *"Behold, the Lamb of God" (John 1:29)—The Mistaken Man and the Unmistakable God*

Romans
– *Buried and raised with Christ (Romans 6:4)—Epigraph*

– *"O wretched man that I am" (Romans 7:24)—The Mistaken Man and the Unmistakable God*

– *Suffering producing endurance and hope (Romans 5:3–5)—The Purpose of Suffering*

1 Corinthians
– *"Faith, hope, and love" (1 Corinthians 13:13)—Suffering's Seal Revealed; The Inconsistency of Man, the Consistency of God*

2 Corinthians
– *God's comfort in affliction (2 Corinthians 1:3–5)—The Purpose of Suffering*

Philippians
– Christ's humility and suffering (Philippians 2)—The Purpose of Suffering

Hebrews
– Christ as the Author and Finisher of faith (Hebrews 12:2)— Author Bio

– Surrounded by a cloud of witnesses (Hebrews 12:1)— Suffering's Seal Revealed

1 Peter
– Suffering refining like gold (1 Peter 1:6–7)—Refined in Suffering; Suffering's Seal Revealed

Revelation
– "Worthy is the Lamb" (Revelation 5:12)—The Mistaken Man and the Unmistakable God

–Christ reigning as King—Triumphant Victory and Consecration to Christ Our King

Notes & Sources

This section honors the voices, Scriptures, and images that shaped the poems. It is intentionally brief—devotional, not academic.

Scripture

Unless otherwise noted, Scripture quotations are from the **English Standard Version (ESV).**

Writers and Thinkers Referenced

A. W. Tozer
Referenced in The Mistaken Man and the Unmistakable God regarding the recognition of human imperfection and the need for divine perfection.

G. K. Chesterton
Quoted in Still, Lord, I Surrender on the nature of hope discovered in hopelessness.

R. C. Sproul
Echoed in themes of God's holiness, sovereignty, and the weight of glory throughout The Revelation section.

C. S. Lewis
Influences appear in themes of suffering as formation, the weight of glory, and the refining of the soul.

Imagery and Historical Practices

Sheep Plunge (Sheep Dip)
The shepherding practice described in Where Sheep Fear, the Shepherd Draws Near—a narrow trough used to cleanse sheep of parasites—is historically documented and symbolically fitting for the poem's theme of cleansing and surrender.

Medical Imagery
References to retinal detachment, diabetes, and physical therapy arise from the author's lived experience and vocational background, shaping the authenticity of the prose reflections.

Author Bio

Drew Randolph writes from a life acquainted with affliction, the kind of suffering most would rather avoid, yet the very place where God has continually met him. His desire is to offer readers hope beyond present pain, trusting that God's purpose often waits just beyond what the eye can see. Drew has walked through abuse, diabetes, retinal detachments, dyslexia, and many daily challenges that have shaped his dependence on Christ. Through every trial, he has found strength in God's Word as it echoes through hymns, Scripture, sermons, and the writings of godly men and women who have gone before him.

Drew is deeply grateful for his wife, Jessica, whose encouragement helped him give voice to the wounds and wonders that shaped these poems. He is the father of two beloved children, Mia and Bentley, who have shown him deeper glimpses of the Father's love. He honors his mother, Patrice, and his father, Stan, whose steady faith has marked his own walk with Christ. He also gives thanks for his brother, Nathan, knowing that families who endure hardship together are strengthened and mended by God alone.

Drew is honored to walk alongside the men of Dad Time, a fellowship where godly brothers sharpen him as iron sharpens iron. Through their friendship, he continues to witness the God who both knits and mends through His love and care.

He resides in Cookeville, Tennessee, openly sharing his faith with anyone whose heart is willing and ear is open. Drew works full-time as a physical therapist and continues to seek the God who sparked a fire in him. Through every affliction and every mercy, he has learned that there is only One worthy of admiration, only One deserving of glory, and only One able to mend what suffering has broken. His life and words point to Christ alone—the Author, the Finisher, and the One who turns wounds into witness.

Acknowledgements

I am deeply grateful to the people who walked with me through the season that shaped these poems. To my family, who cared for me during long hours of recovery and offered strength when my own felt small. To friends who checked in, prayed, and reminded me that I was not forgotten. To my church community and pastors, whose encouragement and faithfulness helped steady my steps with Christ.

I am thankful for the doctors and nurses whose skill and compassion guided me through the journey of retinal detachment and healing. I also honor the voices of godly men and women whose writings, wisdom, and lives helped me hold fast to truth when I wrestled with doubt. Their words stirred a deeper hunger for God in me—a hunger sharpened by affliction and sustained by grace.

To all who believed in this work, offered feedback, or simply listened, thank you. I owe deep appreciation to Ashley Emma and Fearless Publishing House for their attention to detail and thoughtful editing advice. And above all, I give thanks to God, whose presence sustained me and whose hope continues to rise like dawn.

Afterword: An Open Invitation

If you're reading these final lines, I want you to know how grateful I am that you journeyed through these pages with me. You didn't just read poems—you walked through fire, questions, and resurrection hope right alongside me. That means more than you know.

One thing I've learned from the people who have shaped my life is this: love doesn't stay at arm's length. It moves toward people. It shows up in the ordinary moments, the hard conversations, the unexpected texts, and the prayers whispered for someone you've never met.

I want to live that way too.

So here's my open invitation simple, sincere, and without pretense. If something in this book stirred your heart, if you're wrestling with your own story, if you need prayer, or if you just want to share what God is doing in your life, I'd be honored to hear from you.

Not through a website.

Not through a form.

Just me.

Just you.

Human to human.

You can reach me anytime at 931-319-2763.

I may not always have the perfect words, but I promise to show up with honesty, kindness, and the same hope that carried me through these poems. We're all learning to walk with Christ through the fire and into the light—and it's a gift when our paths cross.

And as you go, may this ancient blessing rest over your life:

"The Lord bless you and keep you;

The Lord make His face shine upon you and be gracious to you;

The Lord lift up His countenance upon you and give you peace." Numbers 6:24–26

Grace and peace,

Drew Randolph

Reflections

Take a moment to pause and breathe.

Let your heart settle into the quiet.

These pages are here for whatever rises in you: your questions, your prayers, your gratitude, your grief, your hopes that feel small and the ones that feel too big to name. Let this space become a meeting place between you and God.

What is God stirring in you right now?

(Write freely—let your heart speak.)

Where have you seen His presence in your story?

(Moments of comfort, conviction, clarity, or unexpected grace.)

What do you want to remember from this season?

(A truth, a promise, a whisper you don't want to lose.)

What prayer is forming in you today?

(Let this be a place of honesty and surrender.)

Notes: